# A Fool's Errand:

## A Brief, Informal Introduction to Philosophy for Young Catholics

Matthew D'Antuono

En Route Books and Media, LLC
5705 Rhodes Avenue
St. Louis, MO 63109

Cover credit: TJ Burdick

Library of Congress Control Number: 2018946300

ISBN-13: 978-1-7324148-0-8
ISBN-10: 1-7324148-0-7

To my wife, Emily, who gave me the idea for this book.

# Acknowledgements

It is my firm conviction that no book is ever written in a vacuum. I am humbled to realize the great debt I owe to so many people who have helped me, in one way or another, to write and produce this book.

First of all, I would like to thank my wife, whose conversation and encouragement first gave me the idea to write this book and guided me along the way.

I would also like to thank Dr. Sebastian Mahfood, OP, for agreeing to work with me on this project and all of his invaluable suggestions.

I would additionally like to thank my long-time philosophical sparring partner, Morgan Browning, who has challenged my thinking for so many years.

Lastly, since I wholeheartedly agree with Carl Sagan's statement that "If you want to make an apple pie from scratch, you have to first create the universe," I would like to thank my Lord and Savior Jesus Christ, through Whom all things were made, even me.

To all the people who have helped in so many other ways, and to the "great cloud of witnesses," I would like to thank you, too, and I ask for your pardon in leaving out your names.

# Table of Contents

# Foreword

In the 1992 Supreme Court decision of Planned Parenthood vs. Casey, the majority opinion written by Justices O'Connor, Kennedy, and Souter, explained,

> "At the heart of liberty is the right to define one's own concept of existence, of meaning, of the universe, and of the mystery of human life."

With this one simple sentence, the idea of natural law, which St. Thomas Aquinas says is the participation of the rational creature in the eternal law that governs the universe, was effectively dismissed by the Supreme Court.

The reason for this dismissal is the same reason that a book like this is needed. We live in a secular culture that is motivated not by natural law, which establishes a moral code by which we ought to live if we are to have the fullness of life, but by social convention. This means that if enough people want to do something, then the moral laws themselves can be changed by the state to allow them to do it.

Consider two examples – on January 22, 1973, the Supreme Court decided in Roe vs. Wade to consider the process of abortion to be a fundamental constitutional right. On June 26, 2015, the Supreme Court decided in Obergefell v. Hodges that the fundamental right to marry is also guaranteed to same-sex couples.

In these two cases, the Supreme Court formed a definition of personhood and a definition of marriage that are different from what the perennial philosophy of Aristotle and St. Thomas had long taught us, namely that a human person is an individual substance of a rational nature who is created in the image and likeness of God and that marriage is a sacred covenant between a man and a woman.

If we really do find at the heart of human liberty the right to define our own concept of existence, of meaning, of the universe, and of the mystery of human life, then no standard of truth really exists by which to judge any legal case. Relativism, which is the idea that no absolute truth exists, causes all arguments in favor of anything to be won and lost on some standard other than truth, and any standard other than truth is a falsehood.

So, what is truth?

If this were a book on revelation, we could respond to the question that Pilate asked Christ when Truth itself stood before him on trial. Christ had already defined truth for his apostles as recorded in the Gospel of John 14:6 when he said, "I am the way and the truth and the life," and he added for Pilate as recorded in the Gospel of John 18:37, "I came into the world, to testify to the truth. Everyone who belongs to the truth listens to my voice." The truth about which he was speaking is that God is real and that he has a personal relationship with all of us.

Of course, this is a book on philosophy, not revelation. So, we want to look toward a philosophical definition and say, in the simplest manner, that truth corresponds to reality. That means that there is a reality against which all things can be measured. This understanding of truth was advanced by both Plato and Aristotle, two philosophers who lived several hundred years before Christ. For Plato, we find it in his works entitled "Cratylus" and "Sophist," and in Aristotle, we find it in his *Metaphysics*. While Plato has Socrates dialogue in terms of the correctness of names, Aristotle spells it out rather succinctly in saying that truth is "to say of what is that it is, and of what is not that it is not."

Falsehood, then, is truth's opposite, which is "say of what is that it is not, or of what is not that it is." Our secular culture does a lot of that for the precise reason that it takes seriously its right to "define [its] own concept of existence, of meaning, of the universe, and of the mystery of human life." It says of what is that it is not and of what is not that it is. The definition of marriage, which is an exclusive and covenantal bond between a man and a woman, then, is broadened to include homosexual unions. The definition of a human person who comes into being at conception is narrowed to exclude the unborn.

A belief system based on relativism, precisely because it denies truth, has to embrace falsehood as a standard operating procedure. Such a system has to be flexible in its toleration of any other falsehood that presents itself as a 'truth,' especially where individual concepts of existence, meaning, universe, and human life are concerned. The only thing that the system cannot tolerate is any reality that presents itself as absolute truth since absolute truth necessarily contradicts the myriad of falsehoods presenting themselves as 'truths.'

The statement "there is no absolute truth,"

moreover, is what the author identifies as self-refuting because it establishes an absolute truth that it at the same time denies. Relativism, then, is absurd because the system is incoherent. Because the system does not have within itself enough cohesion for it to succeed, it fails at every single test. So, then, why is it still here? Because it has political power through social convention. Many people are happy to accept falsehood in order to get what they want in life and have a good time.

If you're reading this book, you may not be one of those people.

-- Dr. Sebastian Mahfood, OP
Professor of Interdisciplinary Studies
Holy Apostles, Cromwell, CT

Matthew D'Antuono

# Introduction

Thank you for picking up this book. I am very aware that you had a large selection of books to choose from, and I am grateful that you have at least started to read this one.

This book is not a textbook. In the pages that follow, you will get to know philosophy, the various subjects of philosophy, and the names of a few philosophers, but the format is more informal than a textbook and, at times, a little more inspirational. So, I would like to begin with a story that is about the introduction of philosophy into the world and about you.

In Ancient Greece, there was an Oracle (a spokesperson for a god) at Delphi to whom people could go, wait on line for a long time, and then get to ask one question. The Oracle's response was considered to be the opinion or will of the gods. One day, a man named Chaerephon came to the oracle, and this man asked the oracle a very interesting question: "Is there anyone wiser than my friend Socrates?" The oracle then gave a very interesting answer: "No. No one is wiser than your friend Socrates."

You see, Socrates was not the kind of person most people would think was wise. He was not a politician. He was not a great artist. He did not even go around selling his wisdom as some people did. Instead, he was an ordinary, ugly (he looked like a frog) man who cut stones. He was not even a sculptor, just a stone cutter.

When Chaerephon returned home, he called his friend Socrates and told him about his trip to the oracle and the question he asked. Socrates was angry and perplexed at his friend for asking such a silly question because Socrates knew one thing: that he was not wise. So, why would his friend waste his one question? But Socrates was astonished to hear the oracle's answer, that no one was wiser than he.

Socrates took the oracle's reply very seriously, and he considered it a riddle that he was divinely commanded to solve. He made up his mind to interview the wise men of his city (Athens), and when he found someone wiser than he was, he would take the wise man to the oracle and demand the answer to the riddle.

So, Socrates went first to the politicians, the men who had assumed responsibility for the government of the city. Since these men had taken on such high offices, Socrates thought that they must know a lot about human nature and the proper method of government and what is truly good, true, and beautiful. But when he interviewed them, he found that they were not wise after all.

Worse than their lack of wisdom, though, was the fact that they *thought* they were wise. Socrates realized that he was in fact wiser than they, but only because he knew that he was not wise. Neither Socrates nor the politicians had any real wisdom about the nature of man or truth, but Socrates knew it, and they did not.

Socrates then went on to interview other people who were reputed to be wise: the artists, the craftsmen, and the sophists who sold their wisdom for a fee. The result was the same every time. None of them really had any wisdom, but they thought they did.

So, the oracle turned out to be correct. The wisdom of Socrates consisted of knowing that he was not wise, and *that* wisdom made him wiser than everyone else who thought they had wisdom. Peter Kreeft summarizes it this way: there are two kinds of people in the world, the fools who think that they are wise, and the wise who know that they are fools. Socrates, though he was not wise, was a lover of wisdom, which is the meaning of the word "philosopher." The *philo-* part of the word comes from one of the Greek words for love, and the *–sopher* part comes from the word for wisdom.

There was a problem, though. As Socrates went on his search for wisdom, he ended up exposing the ignorance of a lot of important people. When the mischievous youths of Athens saw this, they realized that they could embarrass people by imitating Socrates. At the end of his life, Socrates was brought to court on charges of corrupting the youth. He was found guilty and put to death. His defense speech was recorded by Plato as *The Apology* (*Apology* means "defense", not saying I'm sorry). It is one of the greatest works of Western Literature, and you should read it the first chance you get. It is not hard to find for free on the internet; Plato's copyright ran out a couple thousand years ago. (I have recorded it on YouTube as an audio book, too. My YouTube channel: DonecRequiescat.).

Just before I started telling this story, I said that this story is about you. It is about you because it is about the beginning of philosophy, and you are at the beginning of philosophy.

You are also one of three characters in the

story. You are either Socrates, a lover and pursuer of wisdom, you are one of the youths who takes up the appearance of philosophy in order to mock, or you are one of those who criticize philosophy as did those who brought Socrates to court. You are a user, abuser, or accuser of philosophy. Which role you assume is your choice. You should be aware of the choice so that you might make it consciously.

This story is also about you because you have admitted, in a way, that you are not wise, that you are a fool. By picking up this book, you have expressed a desire to learn more. That is an act of humility, and it is the same act of humility of Socrates, who knew that he was not wise, that he was a fool. May you find at least some wisdom here, and may you never lose the knowledge of your own ignorance before the great and deep truths that I hope you encounter. The greatest and deepest truths cannot be fully grasped by the human mind, but we can make true statements about them, and we can stand in awe and wonder before them.

This sense of inquisitive wonder is the beginning of philosophy and sustains true philosophers in their quest for truth and wisdom. It should never go away. If it does, then you are no longer doing philosophy, and it is time to get back to basics. "Man by nature desires to know," said Aristotle. When people use philosophy as a stick to beat ideas they don't like, they are not being true philosophers. They are acting like the youths who corrupted the method of Socrates, not because they had an honest desire to learn, but because they had a malicious desire to embarrass people they didn't like. May you always wonder, and may you always philosophize!

In order to begin the journey of philosophy, you have to know that you are a fool. The wise do not need to pursue the Truth, because they at least claim to have it already. Philosophy came not for the wise, but for fools, and the pursuit of Truth is a fool's errand.

*Why Catholic?* Because I am Catholic, and everything you read in this book, should you choose to continue, will be coming from a Catholic perspective. Anyone is welcome to read this book, and I hope that anyone will be able to get something out of it, and any Christian will certainly see eye to eye on most of what I write here. The goal of philosophy is to look as objectively as possible at reality and its nature, but my pursuit of truth has led me to Catholicism, and Catholicism has served as a guiding star in my pursuit of truth. This is "full" philosophy that uses the teaching of the Church as important data and looks for harmony with those doctrines. While my intention is to explain the basics of philosophy in general, I will also outline my own philosophy, which is distinctly Catholic. Roman Catholicism is the most well thought out worldview in history, and it helps to perfect philosophy. Many of my examples and application points of philosophy will be about Catholic teachings, and I will point out how philosophy coincides with and can be used to defend Catholicism.

Also (and this might be surprising to hear if you have bought into popular stereotypes about the Church), Catholicism encourages the study of philosophy. The Church teaches that the mind is a good thing and that we ought to cultivate and learn critical thinking skills. True philosophy paves the way for thinking about God, morality, creation, and other topics important to Catholicism. This is why philosophy is required before potential priests go to seminary. Philosophy is the stepping-stone to theology.

*Why young people?* For three reasons.

1.  Because philosophy is the second most important subject for young people to

learn (the first is good theology), and it is largely ignored by our schools today. Moreover, philosophy is often misrepresented by the "mischievous youths" of our day who criticize religion under the guise of philosophy, and it is too easy for you to join those mischievous youths instead of recognizing and fostering a desire for true wisdom.

2. You are, more than ever before, bombarded with information, headlines, flashy graphics, special effects, entertaining anecdotes, half-truths, catchphrases and slogans, and it takes philosophical skills to sift through all the incoming information to find what is really good, true, and beautiful amidst the chaos.

3. As a young person, you still have the audacity to ask the deep questions and think there might be answers. What is the meaning of life? Is this all there is? What makes me who I am? Is there really right and wrong? Does God exist? What is truth? Does love really exist? What is the good life? Is beauty really in the eye of the beholder? Why do we drive on a parkway and park on a driveway? Many people, by the time

they reach college, think they already know everything there is to know or know that there is nothing to know (fools who think they are wise?). You have not been jaded by false philosophies.

These three reasons also apply to anyone who is "young" with respect to philosophy. Perhaps an adult, who has never learned about philosophy before, who forgets his college philosophy class, or was jaded by an experience with bad philosophy, wants to be introduced to philosophy in a Catholic context. Philosophers of all ages are welcome.

So, don't give up. Be foolish, and join me in the quest for wisdom.

# Chapter 1

## Why Philosophy

*Your mansion*

If you won the lottery and bought a brand new mansion, what would you put into it? You just won the lottery, so money is not an option. Would you hire an interior decorator, or pick out your own furniture? How big would the TV be? Would you put in a bowling alley, pool, or basketball court? Slides and elevators instead of stairs?

Now, consider this. Would you invite people to drop off their trash in your new mansion? Would you create a large door for dumpsters to come and unload in your living room? Would you ask the town utilities to direct sewer lines into your kitchen?

No? Of course not! And why not? Because

this is your new, expensive, awesome mansion.

However, as Frank McCourt's teacher told him, *your mind is a palace.* Your mind is worth far more than any mansion or castle that money can buy on this earth. What do you allow into your mind? What do you expose your mind to? How much garbage do you let in without examining it first to see if it is worth letting in? How many bad ideas have taken up residence in the living room of your mind? What infectious and malicious thoughts have rotted the wiring of your palace? What foul refuse have you been playing with?

Consider this one example. All the advertisements you have ever seen or heard were carefully constructed by very intelligent people to convince you that you need, deserve, or want their product.

## *The role of philosophy*

Philosophy is the extermination company. Philosophy is the interior decorator who can give you the ability to organize and arrange the good ideas in a way that makes sense. Philosophy is the guard at the door who examines the incoming information and differentiates which ideas are good and you should keep from which ones are not and you should toss into the street. Philosophy is the electrician who makes sure that the wiring is correct and that the right switches turn on the right lights.

Philosophy is often criticized as being impractical. Philosophy, it is said, just deals with ideas and makes no real difference in life. What people really mean by this is that philosophy won't get you a job or train you for a trade. And they are (mostly) right about that. But they are wrong to call it completely impractical because your thoughts determine your actions, and philosophy is the method by which you purify your thoughts. What you allow to occupy your mind will overflow into your actions, and philosophy helps you determine the best thoughts.

We all have a duty to engage in philosophy if we really want to be happy. No one becomes truly happy by accident. Wisdom (knowing what is important, not mere factual knowledge) is necessary for true happiness, and no one becomes wise accidentally, especially in modern society. Have you ever noticed how the people who know what really matters in life seem to have a deep-seated joy all the time? Don't you want that? It is not easy, and it might take a really long time, but it is worth it.

(By the way, I am compelled to point out that the intellectual study of philosophy is not the only way to true wisdom and joy. As a matter of fact, mere intellectual assent will not get you very far at all. Living your life according to wisdom is necessary. But true wisdom and joy also come from suffering, true spiritual and religious experiences, and heartfelt practice of the Christian faith. They all lead to the same place, and it is best to follow all these paths to their common point of convergence, but each path shows us a different face of the same thing.)

*Philosophy Phriday*

A number of years ago, in discussing the nature of science with my physics students, I told them that I had a degree in philosophy in addition to my degree in physics. They immediately had a lot of questions about what philosophy is, what you can do with it, and why I got that degree. But they also demanded that I teach them some philosophy. So, every now and then, I started off class with a brief philo-sophical question, quote, dilemma or dis-cussion. Over time, this turned into Philosophy Phriday, where I take the first ten minutes or so of class on Friday to teach some point about philosophy (Whenever we don't have class on Friday for some reason, we hold a Wisdom

Wednesday or Thinking Thursday). And my students love it. I can't tell you how much positive feedback my students give me about Philosophy Phriday.

When people get a taste of real philosophy, they can't get enough of it. Many of my students never thought that there was a rational way of thinking about life's deepest questions. Real philosophy is always marked with a sense of wonder and beauty. Everyone is a philosopher because deep down everyone wants to know. Teenagers are sometimes stereotyped as being shallow, but I know that the depth is there. You just have to know where to cast the nets.

# Chapter 2

## You can't handle the truth

*"There is no truth"*

What is logically wrong with the following statement: "There is no truth"? I realize that you may have heard this statement before. The fact is that this idea is very common in modern society. There is no truth, only what is true for you or true for me, they say. There are no universal truths, only relative truths.

But here is the problem: the idea that there is no truth is an idea that makes no sense at all, and anyone who actually holds to it is irrational. I don't say that to be mean, but there is a major logical problem with the idea, and it cannot possibly be true.

If there is no truth, then the statement "There is no truth" is not true. In order to have true statements, there must be such a thing as truth. But the statement itself claims that there is no truth, so the statement must be false. "There is no truth" refutes the foundation that it needs in order to be true. This is what we call a *self-refuting statement*, and this is not the last self-refuting, irrational belief we will encounter in this book. Since this statement refutes itself, it cannot possibly be true. It is illogical.

We will go deeper into the study of logic later, but here is another example of what I am talking about. Consider the statement, "This statement is false." If the statement is false, then it is true since it is not false. But if the statement is true, then it is false, because it says that it is false. So, the statement cannot be true, because then it would be false, and it cannot be false, because then it would be true. This is another self-refuting statement. In fact, this is not a statement at all because it crosses itself out. In reality, it is just nonsense.

It is the same way with the idea that there is no truth. Since it doesn't refer directly to itself, it is not sheer nonsense, but it is irrational, despite how common it is in the world today.

*What is truth?*

At this point, I usually have a student or two

who is becoming uncomfortable with this idea of objective truth, and out comes the question, "Well, then, what is truth?" It is a great question, and he is not the first to ask it (look up John 18:38). Thankfully, it has a very simple answer.

Aristotle defined truth in a way that is so simple that he used words which are only one syllable when translated into English: "To say of what is, that it is, or of what is not, that it is not, is true." Let's break that down. If something is, and we say that it is, then our statement is true. If something is not, and we say that it is not, then our statement is true.

Here is an example. The statement "This page is white" either accurately describes the page, or it does not. Assuming that we have shared definitions of the words in the statement, we both know what the statement means. If the statement is correct, then it is true. If the statement is not correct, then it is false. To say of the white page that it is white is true. To say of the white page that it is not white is false.

This can be summed up as the correspondence between idea and reality. If the idea and reality correspond with each other, then the idea is true. If a statement matches up with the way things really are, then it is true. So, truth is the correspondence between statement and reality. Since truth is this correspondence, you have never seen, touched, tasted, or smelled truth. Truth is not a physical thing that can be handled (thus the title of this chapter).

*What is reality?*

And now comes the last objection to truth in the form of a question. For people who want to hang on to their idea that there is no truth, there is one last resort. What is reality? If it turns out that there is no reality, or that reality is subjective, just whatever we individually experience, then our definition of truth falls apart because there would be no reality with which our thoughts can correspond.

If there is reality, then we don't get to make up truth. If reality is not a thing that we just construct for ourselves, then we are bound to acknowledge the way things really are. This makes us modern people uncomfortable. We have been spoon-fed the idea that we can be whatever we want and that we can do whatever we want. Being bound by anything, including reality, feels like a major imposition.

Strange though it may seem, truth and reality actually give us freedom. If there is a reality outside of us, then we have a world in which to live and other people with whom to interact. Truth allows us to make sense of the world and make informed decisions. A lack of truth and reality binds us up in ourselves. All we have are perceptions, which may or may not give us any real information. Reality is nothing other than what exists, including you. Reality is the way things are. Truth gives us contact with those things outside of ourselves.

### We can't know the truth

A side-step of the truth issue, which is very popular, is to say that no one can know what is true. This is known as *agnosticism*, which comes from the Greek prefix *a-* which means "not" and *ginosco* which means "to know". There are some agnostics who say simply that they don't know and are searching (like Socrates), but the type of agnosticism being discussed here states that knowledge of truth is not possible. While not denying reality or truth, this belief is an attempt to undermine our contact with truth. The problem with this state-ment is that it, too, is self-refuting; the state-ment "truth is unknowable" is a truth which the person is saying he knows. If we cannot know truth, then we cannot know that we cannot know truth. Even this attempt to get around truth falls in on itself.

To reject truth may be modern, but it is also insane. We call people insane if they have "lost touch with reality." But what is that contact with reality except truth? And what is insanity but a denial in whole or in part of the way things really are? As soon as we become aware of some truth, we must believe it or risk insanity.

*Love of truth*

Philosophy is the love of wisdom, and wisdom is a love of truth. Everyone loves truth, whether he realizes it or not, because we are all made for truth. Everyone is a philosopher. Some people just haven't discovered it yet.

The Hebrew word for truth is *emmett*, and it only has three letters in Hebrew. If the entire Hebrew alphabet is laid out, including the different forms of some of the letters, the three letters in *emmett* are the first, middle, and last letters of that list. Truth is not just a part of what is true. The truth that we are after is the whole truth: beginning, middle, and end. We are made for complete truth.

# Chapter 3

## To be or not to be: Metaphysics

*Things exist*

You exist. You know that you exist because, if nothing else, you are thinking. Something that thinks must exist, because something that does not exist cannot think or be aware of the fact that it is thinking. Therefore, since you are thinking, you must exist. Descartes, a philosopher from the 1600s, made this argument. And it is a good argument. The problem, though, is that you can't get much past that. You might know that you exist, but there is no way to know anything else for sure if we start only by analyzing thoughts. If we start only in our heads and deal only with things in our heads, we will never get out of our heads.

The main point is this: you exist. But even before you use logic to figure out that you exist, you are immediately aware of other things. There are things. Whether we realize it or not, existence is the first thing of which we are aware. If you think about that for a moment, it turns out to be pretty mind-blowing. The fundamental and primary thing that our mind grabs a hold of is existence. That is the common ground on which we meet the rest of the world. Existence does not depend on thought; thought depends on existence. Being is the starting point for philosophy, not just thinking.

### Contingent vs. necessary existence

As far as you can tell, none of the things you interact with on a daily basis had to exist, including yourself (you did not create yourself, nor do you maintain your own existence). Since you and the things around you did not have to exist, we can say that they depend on something else for their existence. To depend on something else is also referred to as contingency, and so you and those things are said to have *contingent existence*.

Let's think about what *necessary existence* would look like. If something had necessary existence, then that would mean that it must exist. It would be part of the essence of that thing that it has to exist. If that were the case, then that thing would always exist, because it can never not exist. My own essence is that of a human being, and human beings do not have to exist. The essence of existence, though, is that it exists. That thing that has necessary existence is God, but we will examine God more later. For now, we will have to focus on the contingently existing things.

## How many things?

So, how many things are there that exist? None, one, or many? After all, you know for certain that you exist because of your consciousness, but can you really tell for certain that this book exists, that the floor where you are exists? Maybe you are sleeping. Or maybe you are just a mind and everything around you is merely an illusion. This philosophy is called *solipsism*, and it is the idea that the only thing that has any existence at all is you.

But let's remember that we are dealing with reality, not just making stuff up or exercising our imagination. We need to look at the available evidence and come to a conclusion. You did not make yourself, so you have to come from something else. Your perceptions are either coming from you or from something else. You cannot create and predict everything that you experience, so you must be passively getting information from something else or some other things. And there is no real evidence that you are the only thing that exists. There must, then, be other things.

Another philosophy of being is called *nihilism* (from the Latin word *nihil*, which means "nothing"), and this philosophy believes that nothing exists. This is a problem because it also means that the nihilist (the person who believes in nihilism) also does not exist. The nihilist argues that everything is just an illusion, but the nihilist cannot tell you *who* is experiencing the illusion. Nothing can't experience anything, let alone an illusion. Nothing is not a thing at all. Nothing is nothing, a complete lack of existence. If you have anything at all that can be described in any way, then you don't have nothing.

Thinking about nothing should help us to realize the infinite distance that separates existence from non-existence. It is not as if existing things were a little better or had a little more reality than things that do not exist. Nothing is not just missing a few parts, and nothing is not just a few days from becoming something. Nothing is the complete absence of anything, including space and time. Anyone who has ever argued that something can come from nothing is, at least, very confused about the concept of nothing. You can't picture nothing. You can't imagine nothing. If you try, you will end up with a blank space, and that is still something.

We wanted to know how many things exist: none, one, or many. If we are honest about the evidence and weighing the facts, we are forced to the conclusion that many things exist.

## Metaphysics

This study of the nature of existence is called *Metaphysics*. It is the most foundational topic in philosophy because anything else that we can talk about is something that exists, and it is sometimes called "first philosophy." Metaphysics gets its name because the book that Aristotle wrote on this topic came after his book about physics. *Meta-* in Greek means after. So, this book was called the "after-physics" or "Metaphysics." Another name for this topic is "ontology." We will come back to metaphysics many times throughout this introduction to philosophy.

Even though we are discussing metaphysics

so early on, do not be fooled into thinking that metaphysics is an easy topic. This branch of philosophy, like all branches of philosophy, can be very abstract. In other words, you have never seen, touched, tasted, or handled existence or the nature of being, just like truth. You interact every day with things that exist, but the topic at hand is not a concrete thing that you have experienced or can ever experience with your senses.

Consider this question: have you ever seen the number two? Perhaps you are saying that you have. Can you point to the number two or make a number two? (I am speaking here about the mathematical number two, not pooping.) Maybe you are pointing to or writing something that looks like this: 2. But that is not the number two. That is only a symbol that represents the number two. 2, II, and "two" are all symbols that represent the number two. Just as "dog" is not a dog but a word that represents a dog, so "2" is not the number two itself. The number two exists only in a mind like yours. It is an abstract object.

Philosophy can be tough because it is like the number two. We have to deal with words that refer to non-concrete objects, things that your senses have never come in contact with. Even though you don't perceive existence, you perceive everything else because of existence. Your senses and the things that they perceive must exist in order for there to be accurate perceptions. Existence is the fundamental condition for perception to take place. The things that are the easiest to miss are the things that are most obvious. But if you miss those obvious things, the rest is disaster.

## Space and time

Two more things are necessary for our senses to operate and these things to exist: space and time. In order to help us think about the nature of space and time, and as an exercise in abstract thinking, consider these two questions: what is outside of space and what was before time?

Let's assume for the sake of argument that time had a beginning. We want to know what there was before time. However, the word "before" refers to a period of time. But if time had a beginning, then there was no time before that beginning point. The word "before" has no time to which it can refer. The word "before" simply does not apply. The question is meaningless. St. Augustine acknowledges that the following joke existed in his own time (400 A.D.): What was God doing before time?

Preparing a hell for people who ask questions like that.

As I discuss the expansion of the universe with my physics students, they always ask, "What is the universe expanding into?" This question implies that there is something outside of space. However, the word "outside" refers to one space that is different from another space. But we are talking about all of space, not just one area of space. Again, the word "outside" has no other space to which it can refer. So, the question is meaningless because the phrase "outside of space" is nonsense.

Space has to do with location and time has to do with change from one state to another or one location to another. And this brings us to one of the primary problems of philosophy:

how to account for unity and change.

Some people before Socrates said that everything just stayed the same all the time and change is an illusion. Some said that everything is always changing, but continuity is an illusion.

## Form and matter

Plato said that there are two things in things: form and matter. The world of the essences, forms or ideas (all synonymous) is unchangeable and eternal. In the world of the essences are the essences of all things: humanness, dogness, yellowness, tableness, cloudness, birdness, etc. The objects with which we interact every day are just material copies of the forms, and material changes because it imitates one form at one time and another form at another time. The problem here is that there is no way for the forms to impress themselves on matter if those forms exist in a separate and eternal world. This philosophy, fittingly, is called *Platonism*.

Aristotle said all things are made up of both form and matter. So, a dog is matter that has been joined with the essence of dog. A table is matter that has been joined together with the essence of a table. The essences remain unchanging, but the characteristics and the matter change over time. The essence of an object makes it what it is. Other characteristics that are not essential to the table (color, material, exact shape) can also change over time, and these other characteristics are called *accidents*. So, as long as a table has the essential characteristics of a table, then it is a table, even though the accidental character-istics of that table can change. This philosophy is known as *Aristotelian* or *realism*.

A third philosophy states that there are no essences, only matter. In general, there is nothing else besides matter. Appropriately, this philosophy is known as *materialism*. The problem with this philosophy is that, as we already saw concerning truth and the number two, there are things that are not material. Even if truth and two don't exist on their own, apart from a mind to think them, they still have some existence.

So, of the three options, Aristotle's philo-sophy makes the most sense. It affirms the existence of all the real things we experience, makes sense of change and permanence, and accounts for how essences and material inter-act.

### Self-evident principles

One last point. As we interact with the world, there are a few basic principles that we know are true as soon as we hear them: every event has a cause, an effect cannot be greater than its cause, the part cannot be greater than the whole, and a thing is what it is. If you try to imagine the opposite of any of these principles, you end up with absurdities.

There is not a whole lot more to say about these since they are self-evident, but the last of these principles forms the basis of our next chapter and the fundamental law of logic.

# Chapter 4

## Let's be reasonable: Logic

*The law of non-contradiction*

What is logically wrong with the following statement: I am not myself today. You may have heard people say it, and what they really mean is that they are not acting, feeling, or thinking the way they normally act, feel, or think. Taken at face value, though, the sentence is an absurdity. And I realize that some people like "the absurd" as style of art, but this type of absurdity is different. This type of absurdity is a denial of one of the fundamental principles of being: the law that a thing is what it is.

As we saw in the last chapter, something must be what it is. This is known as the *principle of identity*. Each thing has an identity; each thing is a thing, and it is its own thing. A chair has to be what it is and cannot

not be what it is. If a chair were not a chair, then it would be something else. It is impossible for a chair to not be a chair. Therefore, if I am myself, then I cannot *not* be myself. By the very nature of being itself, it is impossible for me to not be myself, and it is impossible for a chair to not be a chair.

This is the foundation of the basic and most fundamental law of logic: the *law of non-contradiction*, which states that a thing cannot be and not be *in the same way*. After all, I could look at a piece of paper folded like a chair and say, "That chair is not a chair," but what I really mean is that the piece of paper shaped like a chair is not a chair that you can sit in. The sentence, "that chair is not a chair," uses the word "chair" in two different ways. The law of non-contradiction says that a thing cannot be and not be in the same way; in other words, we have to be using the word the same sense. So, it can be true that I am not myself today because I don't mean "I" and "myself" in the same way; "myself" does not refer to my identity as a particular thing, but I am referring to the way I act, think, or feel.

And since we have already made sense of the way things change, then we know that a piece of wood can be a tree tomorrow and then a table the next day. It is not a contradiction to point to a collection of matter and say that it was not a statue a month ago and it is a statue today. "Statue" and "not-statue" refer to two different times. So, the full law of non-contradiction says that a thing cannot be and not be in the same way and at the same time.

## *Examples of contradictions*

Materialism denies the existence of anything other than matter. But we saw that the number two exists, and the number two is not made of matter. Materialism contradicts the existence of the number two. According to materialism: only concrete things exist. Our conclusion: at least one not-concrete thing exists. That is a contradiction, so one of them must be false and the other true.

The self-refuting statements we looked at earlier are illogical because they contain a contradiction in themselves somehow. The statement, "There is no truth," states that there is no truth. But, there must be truth in order for that statement to be true. So, there is truth, and there is no truth. That is a contradiction. Self-refuting statements either contradict themselves, their foundation, or some other idea that is necessarily implied.

## Not a contradiction

It is important to point out here that there are some things that look like contradictions but are not. For example Jesus is divine and human. This is not a contradiction, because it does not take the form, "both divine and not divine," or "both human and not human." It is just impossible for us to understand. It seems to us like "divine" implies not human and "human" implies not divine, but these conclusions are not necessary. What we have here is a mystery, also known as a paradox. The fact that light is a wave and a particle is also a mystery. We can't wrap our minds around it, and it looks like a contradiction, but it is not (if someone tells you he understands it, then he is claiming to have more scientific insight than Einstein who said, at the end of his life, that he still didn't know what light was). A belief is only irrational, unreasonable, or illogical if there is a contradiction within the belief system. If someone tells you that your faith is irrational, ask them to fill in the blank (because it's really only one blank that is repeated) and still do justice to what your faith actually teaches: "_____ and not _____." If someone wants to appeal to logic, then he must produce the logic.

This brings us to the problem of evil, the only good argument against the existence of God. The argument runs like this: "If there was a God, He would prevent evil. But evil exists. Therefore, there is no God." This argument actually does produce a contradiction because it argues that the existence of God necessarily implies the lack of evil; in other words, if God exists, then evil cannot exist. So, if God exists, then there wouldn't be evil. But there is evil. So, God together with evil creates a contradiction: evil and no evil. But evil is obviously in the world, so it must mean that there is no God.

The problem with the argument, though, is that it is not an accurate representation of the Christian God who does allow evil. The problem of evil is an example of what we call a *straw man argument*, a common logical fallacy. This fallacy involves creating a misrepresentation of a set of beliefs that is easy to tear down, just like a "straw man" is a fake man that is easy to knock over. The picture of God painted by the argument is not accurate. We believe in an all-powerful, all-knowing, all-good God who still allows evil. So, the "problem of evil" argument simply does not do justice to Catholic Christianity's beliefs about God.

Another form that the problem of evil can take is this: "Christianity teaches that God is good, but a good God would not allow evil. Evil exists, therefore God is not good." This argument, again, is a straw man, but the straw man is created by manipulating the term "good". Definition of terms is one of the most important parts of philosophy, but it is one of the most neglected, especially by the mischievous youths who abuse philosophy. This argument makes a true statement, which says that Christianity teaches that God is good. However, Christians don't mean by "good" prevention of all evil. So, two different senses of the word "good" are mixed into the argument. The meaning of the word changes halfway through. This is called the fallacy of *equivocation*. This is a very common fallacy, especially in a world of slogans and catchphrases. For example, the word "love" has been tossed around and so abused that it hardly means anything anymore ("Love is love!"). Pay close attention to this fallacy. It is sometimes difficult to recognize, but it is very, very common.

### Formal vs. informal fallacies

Equivocation and straw man are what we call *informal fallacies* because they do not have to do with the "form" or shape of the argument, and I will introduce some other common informal fallacies later in this book as we go along. An argument is made up of a number of premises and then reaches a conclusion. If the conclusion *must* follow from the premises, then the argument has good *form*. An argument where the conclusion must follow from the premises is called a *valid argument*. The problem of evil is a valid argument because the conclusion necessarily follows from the premises. We call it a formal fallacy if an argument makes the mistake of being invalid. For example, consider the following argument:

If Liz has a sister, then she has a sibling.
Liz does not have a sister.
Therefore she does not have a sibling.

This argument is not valid because the conclusion does not follow from the premises; Liz may have a brother (And she does: me. Liz is my sister.). The premises are both true, but the conclusion is false because of the bad form. This argument commits a *formal fallacy*. There are a handful of valid forms, but they all follow the basic principle that the premises necessarily imply the conclusion.

However, the validity of an argument does not mean that the conclusion has to be true.

The truth of the conclusion depends on the truth of the premises. As we already saw, the problem of evil contains a premise that is false or manipulates the definitions of the terms, so the conclusion is not necessarily true. The conclusion is also not necessarily false. If someone uses a bad argument for some conclusion, it does not imply that the conclusion is false. For example, look at the following argument:

> I am a frog.
> All frogs are mammals.
> Therefore, I am a mammal.

The conclusion has to follow from the premises, so it is valid. But both premises are false. However, that does not prove that the conclusion is false, because the conclusion happens to be true. Even bad arguments can produce true conclusions!

The goal, though, is to produce valid arguments that contain true premises, because those arguments have to lead to true conclusions. As philosophers, we are after truth above all else. A valid argument with true premises is said to be *sound*. Arguments can be illogical because they contain a fallacy of some kind, either formal or informal, and beliefs can be illogical because they contain a contradiction.

## *The value of logic*

As I hope you can see, logic is a very important and powerful tool for critical thinking; it is the arithmetic of philosophy. But logic can also be used in a destructive way. Socrates was the first one to apply systematic logical thought to questions about the good, the true, and the beautiful, but the mischievous youths learned logic to embarrass people. While logic ought to be used to find the truth, it can also be used only to win debates. That is why intellectual honesty and humility are more important than logic. Someone who is prideful and deceitful but good at logic can convince himself of whatever he wants, but you cannot deceive someone about basic truths who knows that he might be wrong and looks objectively at the facts.

On more than one occasion, in math, physics, and philosophy departments, I have heard professors lament the lack of education in logic. They wish that students were taught a full course in logical thinking; it would save them so much mental pain as they read papers and examine students' arguments. The closest thing most students get to logic is Geometry (I have taught Geometry before, and I love it. It is a beautiful subject.), where we begin with a few basic premises and prove the rest of the system.

*Science vs. logic*

Before moving on to the next chapter, I want to point out a mistake in language that people make. I sometimes hear people say, "When you look at it scientifically..." when they are not talking at all about science or anything that applies to science. Really, what they are doing is looking at something logically. And I also sometimes hear people say, "When you at it logically..." when they are really looking at something scientifically. For example, Jesus' walking on water is not scientific; science has nothing to say about whether Jesus walked on water or not because walking on water is a miracle and, therefore, outside the realm of science. So, when someone says, "Jesus' walking on water is not logical because gravity would pull Him down," he really means that it is not scientific because he is appealing to science. If he wants to say that an event or belief is not logical, then he must point out a contradiction.

This mixing up of science and logic comes from and contributes to our modern worship of science. Don't get me wrong; I love science. I think that science is a window into truth about our physical universe and reveals the beauty that God inscribed in the world, but it is definitely not the same thing as logic. Science has to follow rules of logic, but logic does not have to follow scientific rules. Logically, it is possible that the earth's gravity pushes up instead of pulling down. Scientifically, we have discovered that the earth's gravity pulls down.

# Chapter 5

## I am nothing without You: God

*Natural theology*

I was once asked what my favorite topic in philosophy is. It took me a second to think through the various topics, but as soon as I thought of it, I knew it: God. This was a surprising answer to the person who asked the question, because God is always thought of as a strictly religious entity. But philosophy can also give us a lot of information about God, and no subject is more beautiful. We call this *natural theology* because we are finding out what we can about God using only our natural resources. It is very difficult and very abstract because when we think about God we are thinking about Someone whom we cannot fully grasp. Augustine once said, "If you understand it, it is not God." In other words, if you have some accurate, neat little picture in your mind of God, then that picture is wrong.

This is why I agree with what most atheists say. Most of the things that they reject about god, I reject, too. The type of god that they portray is not the God that philosophy and Catholicism reveals to us. We have already looked at how the problem of evil is a straw man, and most other arguments against God fall into that same category.

*God loves science*

Perhaps one of the most common arguments against God, which isn't even really an argument, is the appeal to science. But science cannot tell us anything about whether or not God exists because science deals only with ideas about the physical universe that can be tested by experiment. There is no experiment you can perform to determine whether or not there is a God. By almost every definition of God, even the bad ones, God is not a physical thing that is part of the universe. So, science cannot determine if God exists. This appeal to science is more of a distraction than a real argument, and a distraction like this is another informal fallacy called a red herring.

Since we are on the topic, it is worth mentioning how science is sometimes used as an argument against some forms of religion because there are some religions that officially teach things that contradict current mainstream science, and so science is said to disprove those religions. However, there are no conclusions in mainstream science that contradict the official teaching of the Catholic Church. The Church has never officially taught that the earth does not move. The Church has always been open to the possibility of evolution. The Church has always been open to the Big Bang. As a matter of fact, it was a Catholic priest who invented the Big Bang theory: Fr. Georges Lemaître. Most atheists assume that all Christian denominations interpret the Bible in a 21st-century literal sense. This is another straw man. The fact is that no religion is more conducive to science than Roman Catholicism, and it was Roman Catholicism that gave birth to modern science.

*Necessary existence*

Let's return to the topic of God, and we are going to approach this topic through meta-physics. As we saw back in chapter 3, all of the things with which we interact on a daily basis exist contingently; in other words, they don't have to exist. However, since all of those things exist contingently, they did not cause themselves. But their causes must also have had some cause, and so on and so forth. So, we have a chain of contingent things causing more contingent things. How far back this chain goes, philosophy cannot tell us. Science tells us that it goes back at least to the Big Bang, but the laws of science break down at that point, so we don't know if it goes back further than that or not. One way or another, there is a chain of contingent causes.

It is important to realize that this entire chain of contingent causes is also contingent. The chain of causes does not contain the reason for its own existence, no matter how many causes are in the chain. So, even this chain of causes did not have to exist. Therefore, there must be something that caused the chain of causes and the whole universe itself. Since this thing is able to give existence to everything, existence must be its essence. So, behind everything else that exists, there is this one thing, the very Essence of Existing-ness. This is not just another thing in the universe; it is the very Act of Being itself. And we call this thing God. After all, the name that God revealed to

Moses was "I am." God did not say I am this thing or that thing, but simply, "I am."

If someone at this point asks, "Well, who created God?" we can be sure that this person doesn't understand what or who we are talking about. Since it is the very nature of God to exist, He does not need a cause. He exists through Himself. He must exist because He is Necessary Existence.

I realize that this might not sound like a very exciting God, and it might not sound like the God that you hear about in Church or Sunday School or at your Grandma's house, but remember a) that we are just getting started and b) we are doing technical philosophy. Hang in there because this understanding of God is the real theory of everything (because it explains EVERYTHING), and no topic could be more important to know and think about.

Since God is the source of everything that exists and every perfection, everything that exists participates in the divine nature to some degree. Every object with which you have ever come in contact is a little window to God. You and this book and the sun are all dependent on God for existence and essence. Everything is intrinsically interesting because everything shows us about some perfection that can only be found in God's Being. If you are bored, finding something to do won't solve the problem; you need a change in philosophy.

### Non-spatial and a-temporal

Let us continue. Since the essence of this thing is existing-ness, then it cannot change. It cannot lose anything of its essence because then it would not exist, and it would not be, but it must be because it is the essence of existence. Since there is no change in this Thing, then It does not exist in time; in other words, *a-temporal.* The time that we experience is part of our universe, and it results from things coming into and out of existence, but Necessary Existence is not part of our universe. Neither is Existing-ness something that only lives in a certain location or takes up space; It is *non-spatial.* All of space exists and receives its existence from Existing-ness. So Necessary Existence is non-spatial and a-temporal. I realize that it is not easy to imagine something that has an existence "outside of" space and time. It is more than not easy; it is impossible. But this is where the evidence and logic have brought us.

## *God is personal*

Right now, all we have is this Act of Existing Itself. And, since the essence of this thing is simply to exist, it did not have to create. But it did create. So, this thing, God, must have a will. God must have decided to create a universe. Therefore, this Necessary Being is personal. He has a mind and a will because He decided to make a universe, and He did.

Therefore, everything in the universe receives existence from Existing-ness. All of the action is on God's side. There is nothing passive in God. He does not receive any information. He Himself is the source of every essence, and everything that exists only participates in what it receives from God. Just as fullness of truth, *emmett*, is the beginning, middle and end, so God Himself is the beginner, sustainer, and goal of all of creation. God Himself is Truth Itself. Just as Jesus said, "I am the way, the truth, and the life," and, "I am the Alpha and the Omega" (the first and last letters of the Greek alphabet).

More about the word *emmett*. The letters in the Hebrew alphabet double as the symbols for the numbers. So, the first letter in the alphabet, which is also the first letter in the word *emmett*, represents the number one. In this vehemently monotheistic culture of the Jews, the number one represents God. When that first letter which represents God is removed from the word *emmett*, the resulting word is *met*, which means death. If we take God away from truth, we get death. If we leave God in, we get fullness of truth. This understanding of God as the Act of Existing Itself opens the possibility for a real, understandable, and good universe which is necessary for truth. Since God is the source of your existence, you are nothing without Him; and I mean that as literally as possible. Hence the title of this chapter.

## God and contradictions

I want to take you through one more exercise before moving on to the next chapter. People sometimes ask if God can create a rock so big that even He can't lift it. The answer to this question comes easily enough if we keep in mind the basic principle of non-contradiction. Imagine that there is a rock so big that God cannot lift it. If that is the case, then God is not all-powerful because there is something He cannot do. But God is all-powerful. And now we have a contradiction: God is all-powerful and God is not all-powerful. Therefore, this situation is a contradictory situation and is not possible. As a matter of fact, since it involves a contradiction, it is not a situation at all; it is a non-situation. It is a state of being that is not possible for any being in any universe under any circumstances because they do not even have the potential for being. Therefore, God cannot create a rock so big that He cannot lift it. "Aha! So there is something else that God cannot do!" Nope. God can do all things, but contradictions are not things. Contradictions are non-things; they do not even have the capacity to exist in the first place. This does not put any limit on God; it only helps us to understand what is possible and what is absolutely impossible based on the very nature of Being Itself.

*Making God in our image*

This image we have created of God must be guarded from anthropomorphism. It is all too tempting to think of God in our own image, but that would lead to a straw man. For example, if you think of God as a powerful human being who needs to be instructed by us and who throws emotional temper tantrums, then God's omnipotence and unchanging-ness are contra-dicted. But that image of God is a straw man, however popular it may be. In the spiritual life, it is necessary to use images and analogies to help us understand the heart of God, but in philosophy we cannot stress enough the importance of being strict in our thinking and naming of God. We simply cannot wrap our minds around God. We are limited, finite creatures trying to talk about the limitless, infinite Creator. That does not mean that we cannot make true statements about Him, but we have to understand the limits of our thoughts. Just as modern physicists have equations that accurately describe some very strange behavior of nature that they cannot really understand, so we have accurate philosophical statements about a Being we cannot fully grasp.

This is the best part of philosophy: the part where we reach the limit of our abilities and stand in awe at the Source of all Things. I once went on a mission trip to a country in Central Asia during the summer. At the end of our time there, we went to an empty ski resort for time to pray and mentally process our trip. One day, some of us pointed to a snow-capped peak and said, "Let's go." It took a long time, but we eventually made it to the top, and we found that we were only on the edge of an entire rugged mountain range with snow-capped mountain after snow-capped mountain going beyond what we could see. It is one of the most beautiful things I have ever seen. We simply did not have the ability to go any further. We could not "enter in" to the beauty of that place. We could only gaze in complete wonder at the beauty before us. So is the mind before the beautiful mystery of God.

# Half-time pep talk

The topics we have been discussing are not easy. Philosophy requires rigorous abstract thinking, and it is easy to tire quickly even during a brief introduction like this. We have more topics to go, and our understanding and application of basic principles about truth, being, and logic will be put to the test. So, I thought it would be good to offer some inspiration by way of a story to keep you moving through this point. This is not a story about a particular philosopher; it is a story about every philosopher. It will give you a picture of where you have been and (hopefully) where you are going. It was written as a story within a larger book called *The Republic*, written by Plato (another book that I cannot recommend highly enough). Plato was also the author of *The Apology*, from which we got the story about Socrates in the introduction. Fittingly, this story is also placed in the mouth of Socrates, though it is doubtful that Socrates ever actually told this story. It is sometimes known as the allegory of the cave.

Imagine a deep underground cave with a small entrance and a large ceiling. On the floor of the cave are prisoners who are bound so that they cannot move their bodies or turn their heads. They are stuck facing the back wall of the cave, and they have been sitting like this all their lives. The little light that comes in through the entrance of the cave casts their own shadows on the wall in front of them. Above and behind them is a platform where there is a fire, and people bring cut-outs of all sorts of things in front of the fire, and their shadows are cast onto the wall. The prisoners have only seen shadows in their lives. So, they think that the shadow created by the cut-out of the dog is actually a dog, and the shadow of their neighbor is actually their neighbor, and the shadow cast by the cut-out of a tree is actually a tree. They even think that the echo of a person imitating a dog on the platform above is actually the sound that a dog makes. Since the sound echoes off the wall where the shadow of the dog appears, it seems like the bark is coming from the dog. This, we would say, is a sad way to live. But it is all these people have known. They think they know about dogs and trees and their neighbors, but they really only know shadows.

Imagine now that someone comes and sets one of the prisoners free and makes him stand up. Do you think that the freed prisoner will appreciate this? He has never stood up before. And what if he is made to look at the light coming from the entrance to the cave and the fire and the cut-outs. His eyes will hurt and he will be confused. The cut-out of the dog will seem less real to him than the shadow he has always known. He will beg to be let go so that he can sit down again and resume the comfort-table bonds of his previous existence.

But imagine that the liberator grabs a firm hold of the freed man and drags him out of the cave and into the light. The freed man will barely be able to open his eyes because of the light, and real trees and dogs would be even stranger to him than the cut-outs. If his liberator tells him that these are real trees and dogs, then the freed man will call him a liar. The freed man first begins by looking around at night, and then in the morning or evening, and then finally he can see during the day. Then he finds that he can look directly at the sun, and he can think about the sun and study the sun, and he finds that it is by the sun that he is able to see all other things.

This is what philosophy is about. We are all

brought up in a society with certain ideas about what is good, true, and beautiful, or that there is no goodness, truth, or beauty. So when our previously ideas are challenged, it hurts. We don't want to be forced to see our errors. We liked our comfortable fiction. It is difficult and painful work to purge away our old notions of things and learn to see and reason correctly about existence and morality. But, it is worth every second. Every step closer to truth is a step well-taken, no matter how painful.

Picture in your mind the cave. People are lined up in rows, all facing forward. Above and behind them there is a light that produces an image on a large wall in front of them. What does this sound like? A movie theater? And how often are we convinced that the world in the movies is real life and that our own lives are just a boring copy of the movie world? That the fame, violence, vengeance, lust, greed, fancy cars, big houses, expensive stuff, and excitement are what life is all about? Philosophy calls out and brings your attention back to reality, back to the beauty and goodness of the world all around you.

But "seeing the light" is not the end of the story, neither in philosophy nor Plato's tale. The freed man remembers the other prisoners and feels badly for them. He remembers the misery of that life, even though he loved it at the time, and he endeavors to go back down into the cave to free them. But when he arrives he can't see. His eyes are so used to real things, and the light of the sun that he can't make out the shadows on the wall. If they hold a contest to see who can identify the objects on the wall first, he will certainly lose. Though he doesn't care about their games, they ridicule him and say that he got dumber by going "out there," wherever that is. He tries to tell them about the beauty of reality, but they rise up against him and kill him.

Does that sound familiar? For Plato, this was Socrates. Notice that no one left the cave willingly or on his own. There was someone else who compelled him. Socrates was that liberator who came to Athens to set men free. For us, this is an image of Jesus, the Liberator who came to set us free, not only from ignorance, but also from sin. Jesus came not just to give us the truth, but to give us Truth, Himself. Your life as a true philosopher and a Christian is not going to be understood by the world around you. But take courage. Jesus said that the grain of wheat must die if it wants to bear fruit. You can give in to the call of Truth and let your illusory life of celebrities, entertainment, money, and comfort die, so that you can bear the fruit of true wisdom and goodness, or you can hold on to those things and rot. I realize that neither option might sound very appealing, but you must choose. In fact, you already choose, and you will choose for the rest of your life. Every decision you make is a step in one direction or the other. Even if the actions themselves are inconsequential, how you do them might make all the difference.

# Chapter 6

## The strangest object in the universe: Man

*Man is social*

If someone offered whatever you want, but you could not interact with people face-to-face any more, only through written communication, would you take it? All of your needs would be provided for. You could have pets, live in a mansion, have all of your food prepared for you, go anywhere you want (as long as there aren't people there), but you could not see, touch, or hear another human again for the rest of your life, would you take it?

I don't doubt that there is a small handful of people who would accept that deal. Some may take it even if all their needs were not provided for. But the vast majority of people would find it horrifying to never be able to interact with people ever again. It seems that we were built for each other. As Aristotle said, man is a social animal by nature. It is part of the essence of man to live with other people and for men to organize themselves into societies. It is through this type of observation and reasoning that we can figure out the nature of this thing called a human being.

## The definition of man

At first glance, the most obvious thing about humans is that we are animals. In other words, we have bodies that are born, grow, and die just like all the other animals, so we are in that same broad category with them. But there are many things that distinguish us from the rest of the animals, and all these things are based on one characteristic: reason. Man has the ability to reason.

As we observed in chapter 3, some things are not concrete. Mathematical objects like the number two are abstract. In the mind of man there are many abstract things like truth, justice, beauty, perfect squares, Newton's second law, and love. Not only are these things present in the mind, but man is able to perform abstract operations with those things like arithmetic, logic, composing music, inventing calculus, and developing new systems of government. This tells us that man must have a part of him that is abstract. A purely physical thing cannot understand and do abstract things. The mind is not just the brain. Man has a rational soul.

### Our rationality is unique

Some people argue that computers and the other animals can do all of the same things that humans can. Computers have come to perform arithmetic operations and put logic statements together. Other animals gather in groups and have even learned to communicate in sign language.

But it is important to understand how we are vastly different from either computers or other animals. Computers only perform operations because they have been programmed that way. They do not understand what they are doing any more than a beach understands the castles that children build on it. The famous mathematician Roger Penrose has said that the quality of understanding cannot be programmed into any computer code or equation.

And while it is true that other animals have

social systems, all animals within a certain species organize themselves in the same way. Man reasons about how best to live, and many different forms of government exist. While it is true that other animals have means of communication, all animals within a certain species communicate the same way. Humans have the abstract capacity for language, and so we have hundreds of different languages. Our language also has words for things that are not concrete, and we are able to explain the meaning of a new word using other words. As you study vocabulary, you are able to understand the meaning of a word because of the other words that are present, not because you must see a picture or example of the thing. The other animals that have learned sign language do not have that ability. Man alone has these abilities to do something new. Everything else in our universe follows the laws of physics or the behavior of its species. It is the rational mind of man that gives him this ability.

Some modern philosophers have tried to deny the existence of the mind because we do not perceive our mind. At no point does our mind become the center of our attention. So, some philosophers have argued that man is purely material. This idea of man as material without a soul fits together well with materialism, mentioned back in chapter 3. However, the reason we do not perceive our minds is not because the mind does not exist, but because it is by the mind that we perceive everything else. To be aware of our mind would be like seeing our eyes without the aid of a mirror. In the case of the mind, the mirror is the evidence we have already been talking about in this chapter. All the products of human society are the reflection of mind at work.

Let's take another look at materialism. Let us assume for a moment that it is true. If nothing exists besides matter and energy, then everything and every event is the result of blind material forces, whether those laws are known to us or not. But if every event is just a result of the laws of physics that govern the interaction of particles and energy, then that means even the belief about materialism is the result of those forces. The materialist holds his beliefs not because he has used his intellect and freely chosen the most rational belief, but only because that was the result of all the laws of physics that produced his body and his brain state at that moment. Every decision made by every human being and every belief that each person has held has been the result of the laws of nature. Nobody is to blame for anything, just physics. But, this cuts the feet off the very notion of truth, which requires intelligence. This also contradicts everything that is most evident to us: our intellect and our free will. These are the things that are so easy for us to miss because they are so obvious. Therefore, materialism is false.

The previous paragraph is an example of a type of logical argument. It is called a *reductio ad absurdum*, and it is done by assuming an idea to be true, following the idea wherever it leads, and discovering a contradiction or some other absurd result. In this case, we assumed materialism to be true, and we found that the result was self-refutation (materialism destroys the very notion of truth) and the impossibility of everything that is most obvious to us. In order for us to have the abilities that we so obviously have, we must have a mind.

## Soul-body relationship

Since we have a mind, which is the soul or at least part of the soul, we must figure out if a human is a union of soul and body, if a human is just a soul that lives in the body for a little while, or if a human is just a soul having the illusion of a body. That third option leads us back to the old insanity of solipsism, again discussed in chapter 3, so we will not go into that here.

I want to pause at this moment to point out how important it is that a philosophy be consistent throughout. Every part of philosophy is connected. The ethics (to come), the metaphysics, the theory of man, epistemology (also to come), and the idea of God all have to be in harmony with each other. Philosophy is not a cafeteria line where we decide to have some spicy solipsism for an appetizer, a little Aristotelian realism for the main course, and materialist hedonism for dessert. Everything informs everything else, and the philosophy that most accurately describes the nature of reality must form one single fabric. Ok, back to body and soul.

If the soul and body were separate things, then what happens to the body should not affect the soul. The mind would be able to do its own thing and the body would act like an antenna for the thoughts of the soul. But that is not the way it is. When someone gets drunk, his abstract thinking faculties are as distorted as his physical moving abilities. The mind does not continue functioning perfectly in its abstractness while the body tumbles about. The mind is somehow united to the brain. Man is a body/soul unity.

## *Reason and God*

This abstract nature of human beings is another important piece of data with respect to God. Let's see how these tie together. One of our basic principles is that an effect cannot be greater than its cause. So, a whole chain of purely concrete causes cannot produce intelligence. The bombardment of subatomic particles can never produce a single abstract ability. Therefore, there must be some intelligent cause that can put intelligence into creatures in the universe. That intelligent cause is God. And so we have another argument for God, and it is an argument that tells us something about Him: He is the very source of intellect.

# Chapter 7

## You should know the difference: Epistemology

*Scientific knowledge*

What is logically wrong with the following statement: "science is the only way to know what is true." This statement expresses what is sometimes known as scientism, and it is a very common belief in society today. Many people hold this opinion without realizing it. You may have even heard people say something like, "Well, it hasn't been proven scientifically, so we don't really know if it is true." But there is a major problem with this belief. The domain of science is the physical universe and statements about that universe which can be tested. If you were to draw a circle that represented what science knows and can know, only ideas that can be tested by physical experiments would fit into that circle. However, the statement "science is the only way to know what is true" cannot be tested by any experiment. As a matter of fact, the statement is a philosophical statement about science, and it does not belong in the circle of science. But the statement denies anything outside of science as being knowable; philosophy is not a category of valid knowledge. Therefore, the statement is self-refuting. It is a philosophical statement, but it states that philosophical statements cannot be known. Scientism is self-refuting.

## Epistemology

How can we know things, then? This study of how we know things is known as *epistemology*. We have already followed Descartes' line of thought regarding what we can know with absolute certainty, and we found that we can know that we are thinking and that we exist. But that was the end. Nothing else is guaranteed, and everything can be doubted if we are really creative about finding other possibilities. Is that kind of radical doubt really the best way to go about trying to know? No, it is not, because it leaves us wrapped up only in our own minds. This type of knowing, where philosophers begin in the mind and try to work their way out is known as *idealism*, and it has led to all kinds of problems in modern philosophy.

Plato's theory of knowing is called *anamnesis*, and it comes from the Greek prefix *ana-* which means "again" and the root *mnesis* which means "memory". Anamnesis means remembering. Plato believed that man is a soul that lives in the body for a little while. The soul, before entering the body, comes from the world of forms and knows all the true essences of things. When the soul enters the body it forgets those essences, and the rest of life is spent recognizing and relearning those essences from the things around us, which are only copies of the true essences. For example, before entering the body, the soul sees and knows the essence of trees; the soul knows "tree-ness." Then, when the soul enters the body and encounters all of the copies and shadows of trees (remember the cave?), the soul is reminded of the essence of tree, which it knew before. The evidence that Plato cited for his theory was the fact that a boy could come to learn new things only by asking him questions (see *The Meno)*. By putting thoughts together, even an unlearned slave boy could put together a proof in geometry. The slave boy is able to do this, said Plato, because he already knew these things before inhabiting a body and only needed to be prompted to remember them.

There are two things to notice about Plato's theory. First of all, his whole theory depends on the pre-existence and separateness of the soul. If the soul begins to exist with the body and is united to the body in an essential way, then there is no "before" when the soul could have known everything.

### Deductive vs. inductive reasoning

Also, Plato was using the power of logic to develop new ideas. There are two ways of using logic. One is deductive reasoning, which is the type of reasoning we looked at in the chapter on logic. We begin with some premises, put them together, and the conclusion must be true as long as the premises are true. Plato's example of the slave boy producing a proof in Geometry only demonstrates the power of this unique human ability to reason abstractly. The other type of reasoning is inductive reasoning where we see a pattern, identify the pattern, and make predictions based on that pattern. Most of science is like this, and it never produces complete certainty. There is always the possibility that the next one will be different.

## *Back to epistemology*

Aristotle's theory of knowledge makes the most sense. Due to man's body-soul unity, we do not begin our lives knowing anything at all, but we are born with innate abilities. As we interact with the world, real objects impress themselves on our senses, and an image is formed in the intellect of those objects. Our intellect is then able to abstract the essences of things and their properties. For example, when I see a table, my senses perceive the table. My abstract intellect then takes the sense impression and abstracts those characteristics to form the idea of a table. As I see more tables, this idea is refined. Our mind, then, is able to recognize those same essences in other things and analyze those abstract concepts derived from our experience with the world. As we discover new things, our minds are able to think about how those new things are different from the other things we know. When I see a tree, I know that it is not a table because it doesn't fit with my idea of table. And as we discover different things in the same class, like learning that there are different types of tables, our mind is able to tell us how these are the same and yet different from each other. Lab tables, dinner tables, and coffee tables are all tables, but they are not the same *type* of table. Telling the difference between things is an important part of learning and knowing. This theory of knowledge fits perfectly with the body-soul unity of man and the fact that we interact with real objects, and so the name of this theory is *realism*.

## Unreliability of the senses

Some people claim that our senses and sense impressions are not really reliable because we make mistakes so often. This is a self-refuting statement, though, because if our mistakes run so rampant, how can we know that anyone is wrong in the first place? Stating that someone made a mistake assumes that someone else knows the right answer. The fact that students get so many math questions wrong does not undermine the reliability of the rules of arithmetic. One of my philosophy professors once told our class about a special he saw on TV about how unreliable the human memory is. I wondered how he could be so certain about his memory of that TV program. The fact that we are sometimes wrong only emphasizes the need to check our conclusions and bring in the help of other people. Man is a social animal, and philosophy is a social endeavor.

## Language

This whole process is aided greatly by language because it is by these symbols and signs of words that we are able to identify and communicate with each other and think clearly. This is why definitions are so important. Your thoughts and your communication can only be as clear as your definitions. Fuzzy definitions will result in fuzzy thoughts and fuzzy communication. The best way to avoid the common fallacy of equivocation is simply to ask for a definition. Our definitions tell us exactly how things are the same and different from each other. For example, Aristotle's definition of man as a rational animal tells us what class man fits into (animal) and the specific quality that makes him different from everything else in that category (rational). New words can be invented as we encounter new things, but language is first learned in community. This emphasizes, again, the social nature of man. Everything ties together.

## *Knowing by authority*

Consider this question that I pose to my students at the beginning of my physics course: how do YOU know that the earth goes around the sun? I get a lot of answers about the sun going around the earth, the seasons, the changing positions of the stars in the sky, cloud movement, and all kinds of other ideas, but all of them can be explained in other ways. In the end, they realize that they themselves have no actual evidence that the earth goes around the sun, and that they have only trusted their teachers. As a matter of fact, it is quite difficult to gain the experience necessary to prove that the earth goes around the sun based on your own observations. For 99.9% of the earth's population, the movement of our planet is a matter of faith: we believe what the scientific community tells us. This is not a problem; the scientific community is trustworthy for this type of information, but it is a little shocking to start thinking about how little we actually know for ourselves because of our own reason and experience.

Therefore, another valid method of learning is through authority. The scientific community is a valid authority on questions about the orbit and motion of the planets, so we can trust it. It is necessary to trust groups and people in order to operate in the world. This, too, derives from our nature as social creatures. We were made to reveal truth to each other. Reason and experience point us to the validity of authority.

I should point out that appealing to authority can also be a logical fallacy if the source is not a reliable authority. For example, many scientists do not hesitate to air their views on religion and philosophy. So, some people appeal to these brilliant scientists when denouncing religion or belief in God. But these scientists are not necessarily authorities on philosophy, religion, or the Catholic faith. They may be brilliant scientists, and they would be reliable authorities on scientific questions, but that does not mean that they have achieved true wisdom. Experts are not necessarily wisemen.

This is why it is so important to be engaged in reading great books. We are social beings, and philosophy is best done in a community of philosophers. We obviously cannot talk with Plato, Aristotle, St. Augustine, and St. Thomas Aquinas in person, but we can talk with them through their books. We do not need to invent everything for ourselves. We can check our reasoning with theirs. The image of a dwarf standing on the shoulders of giants was a common image in the Middle Ages. We only are dwarves, and so we cannot see very far by ourselves. But if we climb onto the shoulders of giants, then we might be able to see a little further than they. When we read the books of the great thinkers of the past, we use their stature to prop up our own. An apprentice first has to learn the technique of the master, and then he can create his own style and go off on his own. We are fools and lovers of wisdom, so we gather together with others who share our love of wisdom, even if it is only in books.

We now have three methods of knowing: experience, logic, and authority. Those three resources must be used to know and learn the truth. Whenever we must discover some truth, we gain as much evidence as we can and follow where it leads. We have nothing to lose but illusion and only truth to gain.

# Chapter 8

## Can money buy happiness: Ethics Part 1

*Happiness*

You only live once (YOLO). So, why do you go to school? After turning 16, you don't need to go any more. Most students tell me they go to school so that they can get into a good college. I ask them why they want to get into a good college, and they tell me that they want to get a good job. I ask them why they want to get a good job, and they tell me so they can have money. I ask them why they want to have money (they start questioning my sanity at this point), and they begin to falter. They realize that they want money to buy things, to provide for a family, to be able to live comfortably. Then I ask them why they want all those things, and they really don't quite know what to say. Eventually, with some prompting, they realize that they want all of those things because they think they will make them happy. If I ask them why they want to be happy, they have nothing more to say. Happiness is its own reason. All of those other things are means, and happiness is the end. I then tell them that those are okay reasons to go to school but not good reasons to go to school. We will come back to this later. Let's focus on this idea of happiness.

Is happiness something that money can buy? Money can buy candy, and I really enjoy candy. Candy brings me the happiness of enjoyment. Money can buy me a comfortable house and furniture. So money can buy me the happiness of comfort. Money can buy me entertainment. Aren't those the things everyone seems to be after? Enjoyment, comfort, and entertainment? I hear my students say that they look forward to weekends and vacations for those very reasons. But do those things bring us real happiness? How do you feel after a day of binging on candy and TV shows or movies? Do you feel really alive, or do you feel sluggish and mopey, like a tiger or a snail? What if there was something more? What if there was a better kind of happiness?

You see, happiness is one of the words that

we use without giving a clear definition. So it is really easy to equivocate with that word (use the word in more than one sense). The types of happiness discussed in the first paragraph are types of happiness, but Plato, Aristotle, St. Augustine, St. Thomas Aquinas, and many other wise people discuss a different type of happiness. You might be wondering why we are discussing happiness in a chapter about ethics, but the Ancients, the Medievals, and the Church all say that happiness is the main point in ethics. Only since the "enlightenment" (when everybody went on a diet) has ethics become about anything else. The classical idea of happiness was when a man reached his fullest potential and is thriving. We have already discussed how humans have a particular nature or essence, and a man is most truly happy when he is fulfilling that essence.

Think of it this way. Imagine that I take a guitar and start using it for construction. What will happen to that guitar? It will break or at least be badly damaged. It is bad for the guitar to be treated that way. But when the guitar is placed in the hands of a virtuoso, it produces beautiful music. It is good for the guitar to be treated that way. So it is with the human. When we use ourselves in ways contrary to our essence, we cannot reach our full potential, and we do not thrive; instead, we do damage to ourselves. The worst part is that we also damage our ability to recognize the damage. We become unhappy, and we become less able to recognize our own unhappiness. But, when we live according to our essence, we can reach our fullest potential.

## *Two attempts at happiness*

There are two ways of pursuing happiness. The modern way is to change reality to conform with my desires. The classical way is to change my desires to conform with reality. I can fight against my own nature and the rest of the world and try to bend it to my will and my emotions and my ever-changing wants. Or I can learn to live in harmony with my nature as a human being and the rest of the world. The first way of pursuing happiness is based on the modern idea that happiness is comfort, enjoyment, and entertainment. The second way of pursuing happiness is based on the classical idea that happiness has more to do with my character, my state of being, and being a certain type of person.

Let me be clear here that when I talk about living according to our nature, I am not talking about the individual preferences that people have. (Definitions are important, right?) I am not talking about the way that I want to live my life or what my emotions tell me on a day-to-day basis or what my personality is. I am talking about our common essence as human beings. In the way I am using the word here, my nature is not introverted, likes to read, enjoys exercise, or anything else about my personality. My nature is a body/soul unity with intellectual capacity and a social nature. I have a mind, will, and emotions, and true happiness comes from developing each of those capacities to its greatest potential and making sure they all get along. In other words, though my mind might be as developed as possible (and it is not, I am just saying hypothetically), I am not reaching my fullest potential if my mind and emotions are constantly at war.

This is the basis of ethics because it directs all of our actions. Since I am social and need a community to live in, I undermine myself if I deceive others, murder, or steal. Since I am rational by nature, I have a moral obligation to develop my mind to the best it can be. Since the purpose of the mind is truth, I have an ethical duty to philosophize. Since I have a body, I ought to provide for my physical needs like food, shelter, and rest.

## The good

Consider this question: what makes the bad guys the bad guys and the good guys the good guys? The words bad and good are often a part of ethics, and it is important to know where they come from and what they really mean. When I ask this question to my students, I hear them say things like bad guys hurt people and good guys help people. But the bad guys sometimes have some noble goal in mind, at least noble in their own mind. Hitler, after all, was just trying to move humanity along to its next and better stage in evolution. He did what he did in the name of progress.

Well, what makes something good? If I say that a dog is a good dog, that ice cream is good ice cream, or that a guitar is a good guitar, what do I mean? I can either mean that the dog, the ice cream, or the guitar is somehow good for me. In that case, I mean that they help me to fulfill my nature as a human being and reach my fullest potential. Or, I can say that the dog fulfills the essence of being a dog, the ice cream fulfills the essence of being ice cream, or the guitar fulfills the essence of being a guitar. Good is always tied to potential and essence.

Of course, the first and fundamental good is existence. An object cannot have any other good or even come close to fulfilling its potential if it does not exist. Everything comes back to being. And since God himself is the very Act of Existing Itself, then He Himself is the highest good. Nothing can have more actuality or a higher fulfillment than God.

So, what makes a bad guy a bad guy? He is not fulfilling his potential as a human being. He is somehow contradicting the very essence of what it means to be a human. As social animals, we ought to help one another reach our fullest potential. But when a bad guy intentionally harms others, he does not help them reach their fullest potential; and since he is not living according to his nature, he is harming himself. In fact, the greatest damage he does is to himself, because his own actions determine who and what he is. His actions cannot determine the state of being or character of the people he harms.

The real reason you should go to school is that it is good for you. It is good for your mind. School will not necessarily make you wise; it depends on what you do in school. But school is an opportunity for you to develop that part of you which is truly unique: your reason. Man is by nature a rational animal; man is by nature an animal that ought to go to school.

*Love*

When we understand what is good, we can analyze the various meanings of the word *love*. We use this word in so many different ways. I love my mom. I love my wife. I love my kids. I love candy. I love Philosophy Phridays. Jesus tells me to love my neighbors. How can we use this same word in so many different ways? I love my mom and my kids in the way that is natural for family members to love each other. I love candy and Philosophy Phridays because I enjoy them and I desire them. I love my wife in a way that is proper to the relationship between a husband and wife. While we only have one word for love, the Ancient Greeks had four. *Storge* was the word that referred to the natural family bond between family members. *Phileo* was the word for the love between friends (remember, from *philosophy*). *Eros* was the word for romantic love. *Agape* was the word for self-sacrificing love and willing the good of the other. None of these would be appropriate for candy or Philosophy Phriday. The first three of these types of love indicate a desire for some good. Family, friends, and romantic relationships are all good; they can certainly be distorted, but they are good in themselves. Agape love, on the other hand, does not desire anything for the self. Instead, agape works only for the good of someone else, regardless of how we may feel about that person or the feelings we get afterwards. This kind of love is very difficult, and it takes a person of true character to love perfectly. First of all, in order to love well, we need to know what is the good of the other person. Our study of happiness has shown us that the good of the other is not just whatever he wants; the good of the other is that he live according to his nature as a human. This is far from our modern, mushy sense of "luv". With all these different forms of love, it is all too easy to speak equivocally, that is, to use this same word in different ways. The slogan "Love is love" may in fact be an example of a logical fallacy.

## Application: food and sex

Let's try out this standard of the nature of things with respect to a common everyday activity: eating. What is the nature of eating? If you were an alien race who came down to earth and studied humans and observed eating, what are its essential aspects? First of all, you would notice that food is essential for maintaining the health of the body. Second, you would notice that eating is enjoyable. Those are the two essential aspects to eating: enjoyment and health. Therefore, when one aspect is completely ignored, eating becomes distorted. When people eat for enjoyment alone and they ignore the healthful aspect of eating, they do damage to themselves. When people eat for health alone and endure horrible tastes only for the sake of eating certain foods, then they have distorted the true purpose of eating. We *ought* to enjoy food and eat according to our health. Recognizing the nature of eating is important for maintaining the right perspective on eating. Removing or overemphasizing one or the other is a perversion of eating, and eating will not be fulfilling its true nature. Eating is best when these two aspects are given their due.

Here is another, riskier, topic to examine: sex. I realize this is a tricky topic, but it is necessary. What is the nature of sex? The science and physiology of our bodies tell us that the male body parts were made for the female parts. Their primary function is to conceive and give birth to children. The nature of the female body is to nurture and care for the unborn child inside and feed the newborn. So, the first essential aspect of sex is to have children. Secondly, there is an emotional bond that takes place when a man and woman have sex. Intercourse is more than a full contact sport;

the two lovers are sharing their full selves with each other in a way no other activity allows. A secure relationship is necessary for this type of intimacy to be safe. So, the second essential aspect of sex is a permanent, stable relationship and emotional bond (which we find in *marriage*). The third aspect of sex is the most obvious: enjoyment. It feels good. So, in order for sex to be the very best that it can be, all three aspects are necessary: openness to children, marriage, and enjoyment. Not that you have to conceive a child every time you have sex, but that you are not intentionally impeding that piece of the puzzle. As the intimate bond between a couple and the means of procreation, sex is one of the most good and beautiful things on this earth, and it is therefore very powerful and easily misused. It is hard to distort something that is not really that good to begin with, but something really powerful can be distorted very easily. The best sex is not necessarily the sex that feels best; to focus on this one aspect of sex and ignore or intentionally remove the others is a serious distortion of this beautiful act.

So, you see, philosophy is very useful in helping us understand even things like how to get the most out of eating and sex. The idea that things and activities having a certain nature allows us to be intentional about making those things and activities the best that they can be and reach their true potential.

# Chapter 9

## Living the good life: Ethics part 2

*Virtues*

Since real happiness comes from living according to our nature, we need to understand what our nature is and how to live in accordance with it. Thankfully, the Ancients and Medievals laid out clearly what these aspects of our nature looked like, and they are called the *virtues*. The lack of these qualities is called vice.

The fulfillment of our intellectual nature is known as wisdom, or prudence, and its opposite is foolishness. Wisdom intellectually knows the truth and is able to discern what is good. A fully developed will, which is the rational, or intellectual, appetite, is said to be courageous because it carries out what must be done, regardless of what the lower appetites of the senses and the emotions might be telling it. Another word for courage is fortitude.

There are two vices that contradict courage, or fortitude, and they are opposite extremes. The vice of rashness is when the will acts without due deliberation in the midst of too much danger, and the other is cowardice, when the will shrinks from right action on account of fear.

The virtue of temperance has to do with the appetites of the senses and the emotions. In the philosopher Peter Kreeft's words, temperance is a right response to reality. We like what is truly good and dislike what is truly bad, and our actions correspond to these likes and dislikes.

The right relationship between these three aspects of man is known as justice. When the intellect conforms the will to what is truly good, and the intellect and will conform to themselves the physical and emotional appetites, there is justice.

Wisdom, courage, temperance, and justice are known as the four cardinal virtues. Because of the role that virtues play in reaching our full potential, this theory of ethics is called virtue ethics.

Unfortunately, this word "virtue" does not have the same meaning in today's society that it used to have. Today, "virtue" means sexual purity. The classical sense of the word is strength, vitality, goodness, nobility and character. "Vice" has also been altered to basically mean pleasure where it used to mean weakness, deformity, imperfection, wickedness, and perversion. As these words were distorted, so were the concepts to which they referred. We now live in a society that has little, if any idea, of true greatness of character and moral strength. George Orwell hit the nail on the head in his novel *1984*, the manipulation of language is the fundamental way of manipulating society, consciously or unconsciously.

## Rights

Our nature is also the source of our rights. I sometimes ask my students where our rights come from, and they say the government. But if our rights come from the government, then it is not possible to have rights that are not recognized by the government; for example, it is not possible to have a right to education when the government does not acknowledge that right. So, if we really do have rights, they do not come from the government. Instead, they must come from our nature. Every person has the right to education because humans are intellectual by nature. This was recognized by the Church in the Middle Ages, and the first free public schools were established so that everyone could have an education, not just the rich who had the free time and money for a tutor. Since we have an intellectual nature, and since the good of the intellect is truth, we do not have a right to hold whatever opinion we want; we have the right to pursue truth and philosophize.

Since we have a nature that tells us what is good for us and what is not good for us, the choices we make are based on the pursuit of such things that are good, or virtuous, and on the avoidance of such things that are not good, or vicious. The fullness of our rights is found in our pursuing such goodness and virtue and in our avoiding such evil and vice in everything we do.

Since the nature of a woman's body is to nurture and love her baby, and a baby is a unique and invaluable human being, for instance, a woman does not have the right to choose to kill the baby, which would be an abuse of her will; instead, she has the right to choose to nurture that baby's development, which would be a proper use of her will.

## Individuality

A common objection against virtue ethics (which isn't really an objection, only a red herring, in other words, a distraction) is that if we all follow the same guidelines of the virtues, then we will all end up being the same; a society of people who are all the same would be boring. But remember that the virtues only relate to the nature that we all share, not our individual talents and personalities. Virtue ethics states that the virtues are the basis of living out the rest of your personality. You actually become more of yourself by becoming virtuous. Whatever you enjoy doing, you will be better at it if you are wiser, more courageous, and more temperate. Think of it the other way. Vice actually makes everyone the same. Selfish, prideful, greedy, lustful, lazy people are incredibly monotonous because all they want is money, sex, and comfort. The saints, on the other hand, exhibit a beautiful array of personality and individuality, from the lumbering intellectual of St. Thomas Aquinas to St. Francis of Assisi who seemed to dance across the face of the earth preaching the gospel and serving the poor. From St. Philip Neri who laughed his way to Heaven to the scholarly and hard-working St. Jerome. From the young but the spiritually insightful girl who suffered from a painful disease, St. Therese of Lisieux, to St. Theresa of Calcutta who gave up everything to become poor and serve the poorest of the poor. Virtue makes you *more* of yourself, not less.

## Deontology

Even though it was so clear for so long that our nature was the standard of ethical behavior and true happiness, modern philosophers have introduced a couple of new standards that we have to mention.

The first is known as *deontology*, and is the theory that there is just a rule or set of rules that humans must obey. Whether or not those rules relate to our happiness, we simply have a duty to obey. But if there is a rule or set of rules, we have to ask where that rule or set of rules comes from? How does it exist? If the rules come from God, why did He give them? Either God gave them because they are good, or God gave them for his own arbitrary reasons. If God gave them to us because they are good, then God is bound by that measure of goodness, and God is not really God because He is subject to something else. But if God gave them for his own arbitrary reasons because He is not bound by anything else, then it might be the case He does not really have our best interests in mind. If God does not reveal his laws to us, then we cannot really know what that law is.

I realize that Catholicism might look like deontology, but at its core it is not. It is true that God has revealed certain moral guidelines and laws to us, but that is only because those rules are instructions for running the human machine. God reveals laws to us to guide us to our full potential and become truly happy. It is not as if God created human beings and then some separate, arbitrary law that we have to follow. He created humans, and humans have a particular nature in which they must participate to be truly happy. Since our nature was given to us, the moral obligation we have is really due to God, the Source of all essence and existence, and the Greatest Good.

## Utilitarianism

The other recent theory of ethics is called *utilitarianism*, and it states that right action is the action that will result in the most happiness for the most people. The end justifies the means. In other words, it doesn't matter what you do as long as the result produces the most happiness. The main problem here is the limited nature of man. It is simply not possible for us to know all the consequences of our actions. We do not have built-in happiness calculators so that we can figure out exactly which choice will create the greatest good for ourselves, let alone for everyone else. The consequences of every action go on for the rest of time, and we cannot make that kind of evaluation. We also have the sense that some actions can never be justified.

Imagine that you are offered one billion dollars if you push a button. That is all you have to do, just push a button. However, when you push the button, some innocent person whom you do not know or ever will know will die instantly and painlessly. This person's death will never affect you in any practical way, and you will never hear about it. So, do you push the button?

If you are a utilitarian, you push the button because the death is painless and you can do a lot of good with a billion dollars. But most people say they would not push the button. We have this overwhelming sense that a billion dollars is not worth the death of an innocent person. We are not primarily utilitarian by nature.

(As a side-note, this question and response are a strong argument against abortion. First of all, an abortion does not earn the mother any money at all, and the person who dies is not an anonymous person; he is the child of the woman who bears him. They share blood and tissue. The woman's body was made to care for and love that child. And while the abortionist may make some money, he is taking direct action against that life and putting it to an end.

I was once in an ethics class, and the professor held a debate about abortion. Sides were chosen for us, and afterwards, the professor asked the students who they thought won the debate. One woman spoke up and said that she thought the pro-life side won, even though she had been pro-choice. The professor asked her if she had changed her mind as a result, and she said, "No. Even though I think pro-life has the stronger argument and is probably true, I am still pro-choice." It was at that moment that I realized how strong our pride is, even in the face of logic and reason. Never forget lesson one from Socrates: humility.)

This is why the typical responses about why you should go to school are not the best reasons. The utilitarian mindset is very common today, but it doesn't have a good basis in reality. Going to school so that you can do one thing, and then another, and then another, and then at some point have some calculated amount of goodness in the world or your life is not the best reason to go to school. You should go to school primarily to become more virtuous.

## Relativism

For modern readers, there is one option that is conspicuously absent: relativism. It is generally accepted today that there really are no ethical norms. Everyone can believe what he wants to believe. Answers like this often come up in discussing where rights come from and what makes the good guys the good guys. "What is right and wrong just depends on what you believe." I don't know of any serious philosopher who held this opinion, but let's assume that it is true. If there really is no universal standard of morality, then it is not REALLY wrong to wipe out a whole race of people. Think of the most horrible thing you can imagine. Child abuse. Murder. Rape. Torture. None of it is really wrong if morality is relative. We just think it is wrong because we don't like it, and we punish it because we have agreed as a society. But we have no intrinsic right to call any of those actions wrong if we can just believe whatever we want about morality. When faced with the reality of where their relativistic ideas take them, most people either change the topic or just stop talking. Even after having this pointed out several times, some people continue to say it. But nobody wants to admit that rape, torture, murder, child abuse, and genocide are not really wrong. This is another *reductio ad absurdum*.

## *Chronological snobbery*

One of the objections I have heard to morality in general and to the Church's morality (usually misunderstood) is that it is old-fashioned. In this, they are correct. Every previous age has believed in moral absolutes, and the morality of the Church goes back 2,000 years. However, just because an idea is old does not mean that it is wrong. The assumption that an old idea is a false idea is a logical fallacy called *chronological snobbery*. The truth of an idea is not determined by its age. If anything, older philosophical ideas have a better chance of being true because they have stood the test of time. Watch out for chronological snobbery; this is a very common logical fallacy.

## *The good life*

Ethics is about the good life. The study of happiness and virtue helps us understand how we ought to spend our time and live life to the fullest. This topic provides us with an answer to the age-old question about the meaning of life. What most people mean when they ask about the meaning of life is, "What is my purpose?" The answer is to reach your fullest potential. Catholic author Matthew Kelly has phrased it as: become the best version of yourself. The Church calls it the universal call to holiness and to become a saint. The Ancient and Medieval philosophers called it becoming virtuous and thriving. In the context of Catholicism where God Himself is the ultimate goal, they all mean the same thing. This might not seem very satisfying, but it is, and the evidence is the saints. They pursued holiness with abandon, and the joy practically drips off the pages of their writings and writings about them.

# Chapter 10

# The splendor of Truth: Beauty

*Standards of beauty*

Modern society has a problem with admitting that there is such a thing as truth. Modern society has an even harder time admitting that there are universal standards for ethics. Therefore, it is not surprising that modern society would find it absolutely ridiculous that there are universal standards of beauty. Let me be clear that I am not talking about physical beauty of people like beautiful bodies and beautiful faces. I am talking about beauty in the way that composers talk about beautiful music, physicists talk about beautiful theories, and mathematicians talk about beautiful equations. I mention only music, physics, and math because those are the fields with which I am most familiar, but these standards of beauty can be applied anywhere.

There are three aspects of beauty. The first is known as simplicity or unity. In order for something to be beautiful, it must be a single thing. A story cannot be beautiful if it is just a combination of disconnected stories. A piece of music is not beautiful if it is composed of various different styles and tunes with no unifying characteristic. A theory in physics is not beautiful if exceptions and additions have to be made as more experiments are done. A sense of one-ness is essential for beauty.

The second aspect of beauty is harmony or balance. Beautiful things have parts that tie together in a way that makes sense. If a piece of music has multiple parts, the harmonies cannot outweigh the melody, and the harmony has to complement the melody, not fight with it. The golden ratio was discovered by the Ancient Greeks as a standard for beauty for the way parts of a building or body relate to each other. This golden ratio shows up in nature in the structure of shells, hurricanes, galaxies, and the human body. Right proportion is the second essential piece of beauty.

The last aspect of beauty is called brilliance, clarity, or understandability. The mind is able to make sense of the thing, even though it may not be able to fully comprehend the thing in itself. I find this third aspect to be the most difficult to describe, but we experience it as recognition. It is like when you figure out a brainteaser or get a joke; it becomes understandable, and that is an experience of beauty. This aspect is sometimes referred to as a fitting surprise or inevitability. When looking at a mountain range or landscape, I often get the sense that it *had* to be that way. Leonard Bernstein, the famous conductor and composer, said that Beethoven's music is so beautiful because of its inevitability; Beethoven somehow knew what the next note *had* to be. We may not have picked out those notes, placed the mountains that way, or structured the universe as it is, but we somehow recognize that it could not have been any other way.

### Beauty vs. taste

So, a piece of music is beautiful if it is a single, coherent whole that we understand and has a sense of inevitability. However, a piece of music may be beautiful even if we do not understand it. We may not understand it, not because it is not understandable, but because we don't know the language. It is very important to realize that beauty and taste are not the same thing. Taste is what we are used to and, therefore, what we prefer. So, I may not have a taste for a piece of music because it is a genre with which I am not familiar and don't understand. It is sad that many artists today do not talk about beauty. Art has come to be primarily about self-expression, but the real meaning of art is the making of beauty. Art's most important function is to be a medium of beauty, and beauty is the language that art ought to speak. When an artist tries to make beauty, he will naturally express himself because he can only create from the beauty inside of him; but when an artist strives for self-expression, he will likely produce art that is neither beautiful nor self-expressive. If we put first things first, then we get both first and second things. If we put second things first, we lose both the first and the second things. In art, beauty is first. Although most artists don't seem to talk about beauty much these days, mathematicians and physicists make up for it by talking constantly about beauty. The beauty that they keep discovering is the beauty of pure logic and the beauty of creation, both of which find their origin in God, the artist of creation. Beauty is a pointing finger, and it is pointing at God.

## Love is a sign

Now it is time for our last story, taken from *The Symposium* (The third work of Plato that I recommend you read right away). In this work of Plato, Socrates is invited to a dinner party where the guests decide to compete by composing odes to love. So, the guests tell stories and sing the praises of love one at a time, but Socrates takes the guests off track with his story. While all the others made love look like a beautiful thing, Socrates tells a story where love is not a beautiful thing in itself. Instead, love points to beauty. In the context of his speech, Socrates describes love as desire. Sometimes desire is fulfilled, and sometimes it is not, but it is always striving for the beautiful because we always want what is truly beautiful. In the course of telling his story he switches "beautiful" for "good" because beauty is good for us. What is truly good is truly beautiful. The most beautiful sight man ever laid eyes on was the cross where our bruised, bloody, and beaten Savior hung. The main point is that love and desire are not the final goal; instead, love and desire point to beauty and goodness. Don't be in love with love; be in love with the Good.

So we always desire or love what is beautiful, but we may not always be able to recognize beauty because we haven't learned enough to understand it. This is another very good reason to go to school: beauty. I always explain to my students that I take what I do seriously, and that I try not to do anything for which I don't have a good reason (I am not always good at this, but, by God's grace, I am working on it). The choice to assume the vocation of physics teacher had better have a good reason behind it. One of my main reasons is this: beauty. It takes a long time and a lot of work to be able to see the beauty in physics and math, but it is worth it. I want my students to at least get a taste of the beauty of physics because we were made for beauty.

## Beauty and truth

One of the shocking things that physicists say is that beautiful theories are more likely to be true. One famous physicist even said that it is more important to have equations that are beautiful than it is to have equations that agree with the results of experiments. It is almost a dogma of faith in science that true theories are beautiful. Beauty is the splendor of truth. If we find something that is truly beautiful, then we know that we have found something true. Most of the time, new scientific theories meet with great resistance within the scientific community; it takes a long time for scientists to be convinced of new ideas. But in the case of Einstein's theory of General Relativity, almost all scientists believed it as soon as they saw it. Even though there was little evidence for it at the time and it had not really been put to the test, most scientists knew that it was right because of its beauty.

These standards of beauty can also help us find the true philosophy. The philosophy that most corresponds with reality should be beautiful. The real theory of everything, that God is the Act of Existing Itself, has unity, harmony, and clarity. That one idea is the basis for an entire philosophy, and it is beautiful. One of the titles of philosophy is "handmaid to theology" because we need philosophical language in order to do theology. But philosophy also points us to theology just as love points to the true and the good. Philosophy can be seen as the outer covering of theology just as the tunic of Jesus was his clothing. Scripture tells us that the tunic of Jesus was without seam; a good philosophy is without seam. Everything is interwoven and interconnected.

Beauty is one of the reasons I am a Catholic. The unity, harmony, and brilliance of the Catholic faith astounds me. Everything centers on Jesus. The balance and harmony in the doctrines is perfect. And it is by the Catholic faith that the rest of the world makes sense. But it is not easy to understand. No religion is uglier than Catholicism misunderstood; but no religion is more beautiful than Catholicism as it really is.

*Are we wise now?*

We have come to a lot of conclusions in this introduction to philosophy, but we are still not fully wise because we recognize that we cannot fully understand. There will always be mystery in reality, but we can make true statements about those mysterious realities. Since wisdom is possession of the truth, we will never be truly wise in this life because we will never fully possess Truth in this life. Rather, Truth will never fully possess us in this life. Truth turns out to be a person, and this person is higher than we are. Philosophy is a finger pointing to God. Don't get stuck looking at the finger. Look along the finger to see where it is pointing.

# Suggested Reading

Students often ask me what books they can read to start learning about philosophy. This is the short list.

Plato – Don't be intimidated to read Plato. His works are very readable. He talks to us through dialogues of Socrates, the father of philosophy, and there was no technical vocabulary at the time. Because he wrote in the form of dialogues, in fact, the prose is less dry than mere treatises. Start with *The Apology, The Symposium,* and *The Republic.*

Aristotle – Aristotle is a little more difficult, but he is still very systematic and clear as long as you can pay attention. Start with the *Ethics* and the *Metaphysics*, and use the next author as a guide.

Mortimer Adler – One of the clearest and most common-sensical writers in philosophy. He also had a TV show which you can probably find online. Start with *Ten Philosophical*

*Mistakes, How to Think About the Great Ideas, Aristotle for Everybody,* and *How to Think About God.*

St. Thomas Aquinas – St. Thomas is not easy to read, but he is the essential Catholic philosopher. Popes, Church Councils, philosophers, and theologians have all sung his praises. Even though his work is difficult, it is worth taking your time to patiently follow his arguments and lines of thought. The philosophy in this book is essentially that of Thomas Aquinas. Start with the *Summa Contra Gentiles, The Shorter Summa* and *On Being and Essence.*

You should also read the Bible (start with the New Testament if you haven't already) and the *Compendium to the Catechism of the Catholic Church* (It's the short version – or you can go for the *Catechism* itself if you are feeling ambitious). Reading the Catechism was one of the great surprises in my life. I was amazed at the clarity, unity, and beauty of the teaching, and I was delighted to find that it fit perfectly with where my study of Scripture and philosophy had brought me. After all, God Himself is truth, and philosophy is the path that leads to Truth. There is only one God and there is only one creation, so philosophy and theology (and science, and history, etc.) ought to see eye-to-eye. However, theology takes us where our reason alone cannot go. Our minds can only get us so far, so Jesus comes to reveal Himself to us. Jesus is the messiah for Jews and for philosophers.

Made in the USA
Columbia, SC
11 August 2018